A Giant First-Start Reader

This easy reader contains only 31 different words, repeated often to help the young reader develop word recognition and interest in reading.

Basic word list for *Climb Aboard!*

a	great	swimming
aboard	here	the
all	isn't	this
and	it	those
at	let's	through
boat	look	up
climb	my	waves
down	sail	we
for	sailing	welcome
fun	swim	will
go		

Climb Aboard

Written by Rose Greydanus

Illustrated by George Ulrich

Troll Associates

Library of Congress Cataloging in Publication Data

Greydanus, Rose.
    Climb aboard.

    (A Giant first-start reader)
    Summary: A rabbit and bear have an exciting sailing
adventure.
    [1. Boats and boating—Fiction.   2. Rabbits—Fiction.
3. Bears—Fiction]   I. Ulrich, George, ill.   II. Title.
III. Series.
PZ7.G876C1   1988   [E]   87-19150
ISBN 0-8167-1099-6
ISBN 0-8167-1100-3 (pbk.)

Climb aboard my boat.

Let's go for a sail.

Let's go sailing.

Isn't this fun? Isn't this great!

We will climb the waves.

Up, up, up we will go.

Down, down, down we will go.

We will go sailing through the waves.

Up and down we will go.

Isn't sailing fun?

Isn't it great!

Climb up here.

Let's climb up here.

Look at all the waves!

Look at those great waves.

Let's go for a swim.

Let's go swimming.

We will swim through the waves.

Up, up, up we will go.

Down, down, down we will go.

Up and down we will swim.

Isn't swimming fun?

Climb aboard.

Welcome aboard my boat.

We will go sailing through the waves.

Isn't sailing great fun!